Dad Jokes: Getting Kids to Laugh

Dad Jokes: Getting Kids to Laugh

**Compiled by
Bradley L. Jones**

-- This page intentionally left blank --

Dad Jokes: Getting Kids to Laugh

Table of Contents

-- This page intentionally left blank --

January

January 1st

When does a joke become a dad joke?

When it becomes apparent.

January 2nd

Why should you never buy flowers from a Monk?

Because only you can prevent florist friars.

January 3rd

Why did the dalmatian go to the doctor?
Because he was seeing spots!

January 4th

What's Forrest Gump's password?
1forrest1

January 5th

What do you call a fat psychic?

A four-chin teller.

January 6th

What concert cost just 45 cents?

50 Cent featuring Nickelback.

January 7th

Where do you take someone who has been injured in a Peek-a-Boo accident?

To the I.C.U.

January 8th

Why are elevator jokes so good?

Because they work on so many levels!

January 9th

Why did the cow cross the road?

To get to the udder side.

January 10th

Where does the general keep his armies?

In his sleevies.

January 11th

Why don't fish play basketball?

They have issues with the net.

January 12th

Did you hear about the constipated Wheel of Fortune contestant?

She wanted to buy a *bowel*.

January 13th

I can only handle 25 letters of the alphabet.

I don't know why.

January 14th

Why did the donut go to the dentist's office?

To get a filling.

January 15th

Why did the mushroom have lots of friends?

Because he is a fungi!

January 16th

Have you heard about the new restaurant called Karma?

There is no menu. You simply get what you deserve!

January 17th

What kind of shorts do clouds wear?

Thunderwear.

January 18th

Why are actors told to "break a leg"?

Because every play has a cast!

January 19th

Why do bees have sticky hair?

Because they use a honeycomb.

January 20th

What do you call a bear with no teeth?

A Gummy bear!

January 21st

Why did the banana go to the doctor?

Because it wasn't peeling well.

January 22nd

How can you tell if it's a dogwood tree?
By its bark.

January 23rd

What do you get when two dinosaurs crash their cars?

A T-rex.

January 24th

What did the Buddhist say to the hot dog vender?

Make me one with everything!

January 25th

What's green and smells like blue paint?

Green paint.

January 26th

What's a pirate's favorite letter?

You'd think it's R, but it be the C.

January 27th

Why didn't the photon take any luggage on his trip?

Because he was traveling light.

January 28th

Why did Beethoven get rid of his chickens?

Because all they would say is "Bach, Bach, Bach…"

January 29th

Did you hear about the mathematician who is afraid of negative numbers?

He'll stop at nothing to avoid them!

January 30th

What do you get if you cross a dyslexic, an insomniac, and an agnostic?

Someone who lays awake at night wondering if there is a dog.

January 31st

What do you call bears with no ears?

B

February

February 1st

Did you hear the rumor about butter?

Well, I'm not going to spread it!

February 2nd

Can February March?

No, but April May!

February 3rd

How can you tell if an ant is a boy or a girl?

They are all girls; otherwise, they'd be uncles.

February 4th

Did you hear about the cheese factory that exploded in France?

There was nothing left but de Brie.

February 5th

Why should "beef stew" not be used as a computer password?

Because it's not stroganoff!

February 6th

Have you heard the joke about the bad pole-vaulter?

It never goes over very well.

February 7th

What do you call it when you have your mom's mom on speed dial?

Instagram!

February 8th

How does the Man in the Moon cut his hair?

Eclipse it!

February 9th

What do you call a sleeping bull?

A bulldozer.

February 10th

What did the left eye say to the right eye?

Between you and me, something smells.

February 11th

What do Alexander the Great and Winnie the Pooh have in common?

Same middle name.

February 12th

Why didn't they create two Yogi Bears?

Because they made a Boo-Boo.

February 13th

What happened when two vampires went on a blind date?

It was love at first bite.

February 14th

What did the volcano say to his wife?

I lava you.

February 15th

Why should you never marry a tennis player?

Because love means nothing to them.

February 16th

Why should you never fall in love with a pastry chef?

Because they'll dessert you!

February 17th

What do you call two birds in love?

Tweet-hearts!

February 18th

What do you call an owl that does magic tricks?

Hoodini!

February 19th

Where do polar bears keep their money?

In snow banks!

February 20th

Want to hear a bad cat joke?

Just kitten!

February 21st

Why don't pirates take a shower before they walk the plank?

Because they just wash up on shore!

February 22nd

How long does it take to know if a pair of underwear fit you?

It takes just a brief moment!

February 23rd

What did sushi A say to sushi B?

Wasabi!

February 24th

What did one toilet say to the other toilet?

You look flushed!

February 25th

How much money does a pirate pay for corn?

A buccaneer.

February 26th

Why was the cell phone wearing glasses?

Because it lost its contacts.

February 27th

A pun, a play on words, and a limerick walked into a bar.

No joke.

February 28th

How did the spider find a girl friend?

He searched the web.

February 29th (In case of a leap year!)

Why do scuba divers fall backwards into the water?

Because if they fell forward, they'd still be in the boat.

March

March 1st

What is orange and sounds like a parrot?

A carrot!

March 2nd

What is the tallest piece of furniture?

A bookcase. It's got the most stories.

March 3rd

What do you call a deer with no eyes?

No idea!

March 4th

What do you call a deer with no eyes and no legs?

Still no idea!

March 5th

What do you call a dog that can do magic?

A Labracadabrador.

March 6th

What did the policeman say to his belly button?

You are under a vest!

March 7th

Did you hear about the new type of broom that was released?

It is sweeping the nation.

March 8th

What do you get a hunter for his birthday?

A birthday pheasant.

March 9th

What do you call a lazy kangaroo?
A pouch potato.

March 10th

What is the best way to watch a fly-fishing tournament?

Live Stream.

March 11th

Why was the math book so sad?
Because of all of its problems!

March 12th

How many sheep does it take to make one sweater?

It depends on how well they can knit!

March 13th

Why can't a woman ask her brother for help?

Because he can't be a brother and assist her too.

March 14th

Did you hear the one about the knife-sharpener who quit his job?

He couldn't stand the daily grind.

March 15th

What time did the man go to the dentist?
Tooth-hurt-y!

March 16th

What did the grape say when it got stepped on?

Nothing. It just let out a little wine.

March 17th

What did zero say to eight?

Nice belt!

March 18th

Why do mathematicians like parks?

Because of all the natural logs.

March 19th

Why didn't the sun go to college?

Because it already had a million degrees!

March 20th

Want to hear a sodium joke?

Na.

March 21st

How do you know when the moon is broke?

When it is down to its last quarter!

March 22nd

What's the best way to send God a message?

By knee-mail!

March 23rd

Why don't seagulls fly over the bay?

Because then they'd be bay-gulls.

March 24th

Why did the golfer wear two pairs of pants?

In case he got a hole in one!

March 25th

Why are football stadiums so cool?

Because every seat has a fan in it!

March 26th

What is the loudest pet you can get?

A trumpet!

March 27th

What did one Russian say to the other?

I have no idea. I don't speak Russian!

March 28th

Did you see the movic about the hotdog?

It was an Oscar wiener.

March 29th

What is the Easter Bunny's favorite genre of music?

Hip-hop!

March 30th

What's the Easter Bunny's favorite restaurant?

IHOP!

March 31st

What kind of sports car does a cat drive?

A Furrari!

April

April 1st

What monster plays the most April Fools jokes?

Prankenstein!

April 2nd

Why do melons have weddings?

Because they cantaloupe.

April 3rd

When is a door not a door?

When it is ajar.

April 4th

What is the advantage of living in Switzerland?

The flag is a big plus.

April 5th

What day does an Easter egg dislike the most?

Fry-day!

April 6th

Why do you never see elephants hiding in trees?

Because they are so good at it!

April 7th

What do you call a cat that gets anything it wants?

Purrr-suasive.

April 8th

All the lamps were stolen from my house.

I know I should be more upset, but I'm absolutely delighted.

April 9th

Why didn't the boy like the Russian nesting dolls?

Because they were so full of themselves!

April 10th

Did you hear the one about the mime who went shopping?

He only bought unmentionables.

April 11th

Why couldn't the astronaut book a room on the moon?

Because it was full!

April 12th

What do you get when you cross an apple with a shellfish?

A crab apple!

April 13th

Why should you always borrow money from a pessimist?

Because they won't expect it back!

April 14th

What do scientists use to freshen their breath?

Experi-mints!

April 15th

What is the difference between ignorance and apathy?

I don't know and I don't care.

April 16th

What did one lightning bolt say to the other lightning bolt?

Your shocking!

April 17th

What did one raindrop say to the other?

Two is company; Three is a cloud.

April 18th

The same bike tries to run me down every day.

Sounds like a vicious cycle....

April 19th

If H_2O is the formula for water, what is the formula for ice?

H_2O cubed.

April 20th

What did the parents say when they heard Oxygen and Magnesium were going to get married?

OMg

April 21st

Why did the two fours skip lunch?

They already 8!

April 22nd

What do you call strawberries playing a guitar?

A jam session!

April 23rd

What do you call a dumb carnivore?

A meathead!

April 24th

What is the difference between a well-dressed man on a tricycle and a poorly dressed man on a bicycle?

Attire!

April 25th

What did Al Gore play on his guitar?

An Algorithm.

April 26th

Why are chemists great for solving problems?

They have all the solutions!

April 27th

What do a dog and a phone have in common?

They both have collar ID.

April 28th

What did the cat say when his friend asked if he was lying?

I'm not kitten you!

April 29th

What happens when an artist has trouble finding inspiration?

They draw a blank!

April 30th

Those who get too big for their britches...

will be exposed in the end.

May

May 1st

Why did the old man fall into the well?

Because he couldn't see that well!

May 2nd

What did the big flower say to the little flower?

Hi Bud!

May 3rd

What is Yoda's advice when it come to going to the bathroom?

Doo-doo or doo-doo-not do.

May 4th

How long has Anakin Skywalker been evil?

Since the Sith Grade.

May 5th

How many tickles does it take to make an octopus laugh?

Ten-tickles.

May 6th

How does a meteorologist go up a mountain?

They climate.

May 7th

Why are cemeteries great places to write stories?

Because they have so many plots!

May 8th

Before my surgery, the anesthesiologist offered to knock me out with gas or a boat paddle...

It was an ether/oar situation

May 9th

Why are skeletons so easy going?

Because nothing gets under their skin.

May 10th

Did you hear about the identical twins who robbed a bank?

After they were caught, they finished each other's sentences.

May 11th

Why should the number 288 never be mentioned?

Because it is two gross!

May 12th

Why are stars like false teeth?

They both come out at night.

May 13th

What do you get when you cross a joke with a rhetorical question?

May 14th

What do you call cheese that isn't yours?

Nacho cheese.

May 15th

Why did the children call St. Nick "Santa Caus"?

Because there was Noel!

May 16th

Why do cows have horns?

Because their bells don't work.

May 17th

Which trigonometry functions do farmers like best?

Swine and cowswine.

May 18th

Did you hear the one about the 500-pound cartoon?

He was overdrawn.

May 19th

Did you hear about the dyslexic devil worshipper?

He sold his soul to Santa.

May 20th

What do you call an Amish guy with his hands in a horse's mouth?

A mechanic.

May 21st

Why did the math student do his multiplication problems on the floor?

His teacher told him not to use tables!

May 22nd

Why do hummingbirds hum?

Because they can't remember the words!

May 23rd

What kind of coat is always wet when you put it on?

A coat of paint!

May 24th

What do you call a number that can't keep still?

A roamin' numeral.

May 25th

What do you call it when a cat wins first place at a dog show?

A cat-has-trophy!

May 26th

Why aren't horses good dancers?

Because they have two left feet!

May 27th

Why are frogs so happy?

They eat whatever bugs them.

May 28th

What did the schizophrenic bookkeeper say?

I hear invoices!

May 29th

What kind of exercises do lazy people do?

Diddly-squats.

May 30th

Why should you never give Elsa a balloon?

Because she will let it go!

May 31st

What do you call a group of killer whales playing instruments?

An Orca-stra.

June

June 1st

Want to hear a joke about construction?

I'm still working on it!

June 2nd

Why do trees look suspicious on sunny days?

Because they seem a little shady!

June 3rd

Why do crabs never give to charity?
Because they are shellfish.

June 4th

Where do sheep go on vacation?
The Baaa-hamas!

June 5th

What do you call someone with no body and no nose?

Nobody knows.

June 6th

What does a mermaid use to call her friends?

A shell phone!

June 7th

Did you hear about the statistician who drowned crossing a river?

It was three feet deep on average.

June 8th

Which thrill ride does a wine glass love to go on the most?

A coaster!

June 9th

What did the doctor tell her invisible patient?
I can't see you today!

June 10th

What is a cat's favorite color?
Purrrple.

June 11th

What do you call a herd of cows with a sense of humor?

Laughing stock.

June 12th

I just wrote a song about a tortilla.

Actually, it is more of a wrap.

June 13th

How do you keep intruders out of a castle made of cheese?

Moatzarella!

June 14th

What do you call a duck that loves to make jokes?

A wise-quacker!

June 15th

What do you call mac 'n' cheese that gets all up in your face?

Too close for comfort food.

June 16th

What do you call a parade of rabbits hopping backwards?

A receding hare-line!

June 17th

Why does yogurt love going to museums?

Because it is cultured!

June 18th

What do you do when life give you melons?

See a doctor because you're probably dyslexic.

June 19th

Why did the dieter go to the paint store?

Because he wanted to get thinner.

June 20th

What lies at the bottom of the ocean and twitches?

A nervous wreck.

June 21st

How do you turn root beer into just beer?
Put it in a square glass!

June 22nd

How do you make a tissue dance?

Put a little boogie into it!

June 23rd

What is the last part of your body to stop working when you die?

Your pupils. They dilate.

June 24th

How much room should you give a fungi to grow?

As mushroom as possible.

June 25th

Did you hear about the semicolon that broke the law?

It was given two consecutive sentences.

June 26th

Old mathematicians never die...

They just lose some of their functions.

June 27th

Have you heard about the new pirate movie?

It's rated aarrgh because of all the booty!

June 28th

How did the two dead brothers do in the race?

They were dead even?

June 29th

What do you call a thieving alligator?
A Crookodile.

June 30th

Why did the coffee file a police report?
Because it got mugged.

July

July 1st

Did you hear about the Italian chef who died?

He pasta way.

July 2nd

Which US state is famous for its extra-small sodas?

Minnesota!

July 3rd

What kind of tree fits in your hand?

A palm tree!

July 4th

What did the baby corn say to the mama corn?

Where's popcorn?

July 5th

Why couldn't the bicycle stand up by itself?

Because it was two tired.

July 6th

What is the difference between a piano and a fish?

You can tune a piano, but you can't tuna fish.

July 7th

What did the ocean say to the shore?

Nothing, it just waved.

July 8th

What animal is always at a baseball game?

A bat!

July 9th

What do ghosts like to eat in the summer?

I Scream!

July 10th

Why is "dark" spelled with a K instead of a C?

Because you can't C in the dark.

July 11th

Why did the elephant get kicked out of the pool?

He kept dropping his trunks.

July 12th

Why are mountains the funniest place to vacation

Because they are hill-arious.

July 13th

What do you call a man with no arms and no legs lying in front of your door?

Matt.

July 14th

Why was the dog cut from the track team?

He was a bit husky.

July 15th

What do you get if you cross an angry sheep and an upset cow?

An animal that's in a baaaaaaad moooood.

July 16th

How do you get a farm girl to like you? A tractor.

July 17th

What did the drummer call his twin baby girls?

Anna one, Anna two.

July 18th

Why can't you hear a pterodactyl go to the bathroom?

Because the P is silent.

July 19th

What sound does a 747 make when it bounces?

Boeing, Boeing, Boeing.

July 20th

What did the horse say after it tripped?

"Help! I've fallen, and I can't giddyup!"

July 21st

What do you call a snowman in July?
A puddle.

July 22nd

What do you call a lonely cheese?
Provolone.

July 23rd

How did the telephone propose to its girlfriend?

He gave her a ring.

July 24th

Why is "Fortnite" a bad name for a computer game?

Because it is too weak.

July 25th

Why do nurses carry red pens?

So they can draw blood.

July 26th

What do prisoners use to call each other?

Cell phones.

July 27th

Have you heard the new band 1023MB?

They are good, but they haven't got a gig yet.

July 28th

What does an angry pepper do?

It gets jalapeno your face.

July 29th

You're an American when you go into the bathroom. You're an American when you leave the bathroom. What are you while you are in the bathroom?

European.

July 30th

Why did the Clydesdale give the pony a glass of water?

Because he was a little horse.

July 31st

What is Beethoven's favorite fruit?
A ba-na-na-na.

August

August 1st

Why is Peter Pan always flying?

Because he Neverlands.

August 2nd

What's black, red, black, red, black, red, black, red?

A zebra with a sunburn.

August 3rd

What do you call it when a mad cow gets loose?

Udder destruction.

August 4th

What did the watermelon say to the cantaloupe?

You're one in a melon.

August 5th

Why can't you be friends with a squirrel?

Because they drive everyone nuts!

August 6th

Why did Mickey Mouse want to become an astronaut?

So he could visit Pluto!

August 7th

Why was the math book sad?

Because it had so many problems.

August 8th

Why are Saturday and Sunday the strongest days of the week?

Because the others are weekdays.

August 9th

What do you call an iPhone that isn't joking around?

Dead Siri-ous.

August 10th

What is a lion's favorite Christmas song?

Jungle Bells!

August 11th

Did you hear that NASA has launched several cows into orbit?

It was the herd shot around the world.

August 12th

What does a clam do on his birthday?

He shellabrates!

August 13th

Why do chicken coops have two doors?

Because if they had four doors, they would be chicken sedans!

August 14th

Why should you never tell a secret on a farm?

Because the potatoes have eyes and the corn has ears.

August 15th

What do you get from a pampered cow?
Spoiled milk!

August 16th

How do you get down from an elephant?

You don't. You get down from a goose!

August 17th

Why couldn't the sesame seed leave the casino?

Because he was on a roll!

August 18th

Why did the tomato blush?

Because it saw the salad dressing.

August 19th

What is the worst part about movie theater candy prices?

They are always raisinet.

August 20th

What do you get when you play Tug-of-War with a pig?

Pulled pork!

August 21st

What did the hotdog say when his friend passed him in the race?

Wow! I relish the fact that you've mustard the strength to ketchup to me!

August 22nd

How do you organize an outer space party?

You planet.

August 23rd

Why doesn't McDonalds sell escargot?

It's not fast food!

August 24th

which dessert is perfect for eating in bed?

A sheet cake!

August 25th

What's a tree's favorite soda?

Root beer!

August 26th

How do you keep a bagel from getting away?

Put lox on it!

August 27th

Did you hear about the two peanuts walking through town?

One was a salted!

August 28th

What did the numerator say to the denominator when they broke up?

I'm so over you!

August 29th

What did one pickle say to the other pickle who kept complaining?

Dill with it!

August 30th

I dislike jokes about German sausages.

They are the wurst.

August 31st

What kind of magic do cows believe in?

MooDoo.

September

September 1st

What do you call a guy with rubber toes?

Roberto.

September 2nd

Why did the picture go to jail?

Because it was framed.

September 3rd

What do you call a mischievous egg?

A practical yoker!

September 4th

There were 10 cats in a boat, and one jumped out. How many were left?

None. They were a bunch of copycats!

September 5th

What happened when one cannibal arrived late to the dinner party?

He got the cold shoulder.

September 6th

Why was six afraid of seven?

Because seven ate nine!

September 7th

Why did the bacteria cross the microscope?

To get to the other slide!

September 8th

What do you call an elephant that doesn't matter?

An irrelephant.

September 9th

A farmer counted 196 cows in the field. But, when he rounded them up, he had 200!

September 10th

How many telemarketers does it take to change a light-bulb?

Just one, but they have to do it while you are eating dinner.

September 11th

How many teenagers does it take to change a lightbulb?

Whatever.

September 12th

Have you heard of the group Cellophane?

They mostly wrap.

September 13th

What did the mama cow say to the baby cow?

It's pasture bedtime.

September 14th

What did the bald man exclaim when he received a comb for a present?

I'll never part with it!

September 15th

What did the doctor say to the man who swallowed all the Scrabble tiles?

It will work itself out, just not in so many words.

September 16th

Why were all the ink spots crying?

Their father was in the pen.

September 17th

Why do Calculus majors never throw house parties?

Because you should never drink and derive!

September 18th

Why can't you explain puns to kleptomaniacs?

They always take things literally.

September 19th

Did you hear about the two psychiatrists who passed each other on a walk?

One said to the other, "You're fine, how am i?"

September 20th

To the person that stole my antidepressants...

I hope you're happy now!

September 21st

Why does a milking stool only have three legs?

Because the cow has the utter.

September 22nd

What do you call someone that can't stick to a diet?

A desserter.

September 23rd

What has T in the beginning, T in the middle, and T at the end?

A teapot.

September 24th

My mother asked me to hand out invitations for my brother's surprise birthday party.

That's when I realized he was her favorite twin.

September 25th

What do you call a Fish with no eye?

Fsh.

September 26th

I called the spiritual leader of Tibet, and he sent me a goat with a long neck.

Turns out I phoned dial-a-llama.

September 27th

Did you hear about the giant that threw up? It's all over town!

September 28th

How does Moses make tea?
He brews.

September 29th

What did one fish in a tank ask the other fish?

Do you know how to drive this thing?

September 30th

What do you call a cat that gets caught by law enforcement?

The purrpatrator.

October

October 1st

What's a ninja's favorite shoes?

Sneakers.

October 2nd

Why are koalas not actual bears?

Because they don't meet the koalifications.

October 3rd

What do you call a bee that can't make up its mind?

A Maybe.

October 4th

What's brown and sticky?

A stick.

October 5th

Why did the PowerPoint Presentation cross the road?

To get to the other slide.

October 6th

Why did the man get fired from the keyboard factory?

He wasn't putting in enough shifts.

October 7th

Did you hear about the cell phones that got married?

The wedding was terrible, but the reception was terrific!

October 8th

What do you call a cow you can't see?

Camooflauged.

October 9th

What job did the frog have at the hotel?
A bellhop!

October 10th

Why was the belt sent to jail?
For holding up a pair of pants!

October 11th

How many apples grow on a tree?
All of them.

October 12th

Why did the poor man sell yeast?
To raise some dough!

October 13th

How much did the pirate pay for his peg and hook?
He paid an arm and a leg!

October 14th

Do you think glass coffins would be a success?

Remains to be seen.

October 15th

Why did the pig get hired by the restaurant? Because he was really good at bacon!

October 16th

What do witches ask for at a hotel?
Broom service!

October 17th

How do you fix a broken Jack-o-lantern?

You use a pumpkin patch!

October 18th

Did you hear about the kid napping at school?

It's okay. He woke up.

October 19th

What has a hundred ears but can't hear a thing?

A cornfield!

October 20th

What does a ghost call its mom and dad?

His transparents!

October 21st

What is a vampire's favorite fruit?

A neck-tarine!

October 22nd

Why was the broom late for school?
It overswept!

October 23rd

What do you get when you cross a snowman with a vampire?

Frostbite.

October 24th

Did you hear about the man who stole a calendar?

He got twelve months!

October 25th

Did you hear about FedEx and UPS merging?

They are going to go by the name Fed-Up from now on.

October 26th

What's a vegetarian zombie eat?

GRRRRRAAAAAAAIIIINNNS!

October 27th

Why are skeletons so calm?

Because nothing gets under their skin.

October 28th

Why did the graveyard look overcrowded?

Because people were dying to get in.

October 29th

Why did the invisible man turn down the job offer?

Because he couldn't see himself doing it!

October 30th

What do you call a zombie with a hickey?

A necromancer.

October 31st

Why don't skeletons ever go trick or treating?

Because they have no body to go with.

November

November 1st

Did you hear about the guy who invented Lifesavers?

They say he made a mint.

November 2nd

Why can't you trust atoms?

Because they make up everything.

November 3rd

What key has legs and can't open a lock?

A Turkey.

November 4th

Why did the teddy bear say no to dessert?

Because it was stuffed!

November 5th

What do you call it when two rock guitars accidentally crash into each other?

A Fender bender!

November 6th

Do you know what stinks about a pirate ship?

The poop deck!

November 7th

Which side of a duck has the most feathers?

The outside!

November 8th

What do you call a T-Rex that's been beaten up?

Dino-sore!

November 9th

Why can't your nose be 12 inches long?

Because then it would be a foot!

November 10th

What did the ax murder say to the judge?

It was an axe-ident!

November 11th

What did the red light say to the green light?

Don't look! I'm changing!

November 12th

Did you hear about the restaurant on the moon?

Great food, but no atmosphere!

November 13th

Why should you sit in the corner if you get cold?

Because most corners are 90 degrees!

November 14th

Why was the dead man not courageous?

Because he had cold feet!

November 15th

Someone stole the wheels off all the police cars!

The cops are working on solving who did it - tirelessly!

November 16th

Did you hear about the actor who fell through the floorboards?

He was just going through a stage!

November 17th

What has two butts and kills people?

An assassin.

November 18th

Did you hear about the two guys that stole a calendar?

They each got six months!

November 19th

Why should you save your pennies?

Because it makes good cents!

November 20th

What do you get if you cross a cat with Father Christmas?

Santa Claws!

November 21st

Which weighs more, a gallon of water or a gallon of butane?

The water. Butane is a lighter fluid.

November 22nd

What is the most musical part of a turkey?

The drumstick!

November 23rd

What do you get if you cross a turkey with a ghost?

A poultrygeist!

November 24th

What do you get if you divide the circumference of a Jack-o-lantern pie by its diameter?

A pumpkin Pi.

November 25th

What smells the best at a Thanksgiving dinner?

Your nose!

November 26th

What is the best way to stuff a turkey?

Feed him lots of pizza and cake!

November 27th

If pilgrims travel on the Mayflower, then what do college students travel on?

Scholar ships!

November 28th

Why should you not buy Velcro?

Because it is a total rip off!

November 29th

A bear walks into a bar and says, "Give me a whisky and.....cola." "Why the big pause?" asks the bartender.

The bear shrugged. "I'm not sure; I was born with them."

November 30th

What is the least spoken language in the world?

Sign language.

December

December 1st

How does a penguin build its house?

Igloos it together!

December 2nd

Where do Russians get milk?

From Mos-cows.

December 3rd

Why can't a cow become a detective?

Because they refuse to go on steak-outs!

December 4th

Why are North Koreans the best at geometry?

Because they've got a Supreme Ruler.

December 5th

What do you call a fake noodle?

An impasta.

December 6th

Why is it pointless to play hide and seek with mountain ranges?

They peak.

December 7th

What do you call a cow with two legs?

Lean beef.

December 8th

What do you call a cow with no legs?

Ground beef!

December 9th

What is the difference between a wasp and a fly?

A wasp can fly, but a fly can't wasp.

December 10th

What do you call friends that love math?

Algebros!

December 11th

How do you put a baby alien to sleep?

You rocket.

December 12th

What is the blood type of Autocorrect?

Typo Negative.

December 13th

What do you call an everyday potato?

A commentator.

December 14th

What do you call a pig that does karate?

A pork chop!

December 15th

A bartender says, "we don't serve time travelers in here."

A time traveler walks into a bar.

December 16th

Why did the chicken cross the road?

To show the opossum that it could be done.

December 17th

Why are eggs not into jokes?

Because they could crack up.

December 18th

What is the medical term for owning too many dogs?

Roverdose!

December 19th

What tea can vary in taste from bitter to sweet?

Realitea.

December 20th

What do you call an egg from outer space?

An Egg-stra terrestrial!

December 21st

Did you hear about the circus fire?
It was in tents.

December 22nd

What do you call a snowman with a six pack?

An abdominal snowman.

December 23rd

What is St. Nicholas' favorite measurement in the metric system?

The Santameter!

December 24th

What do Santa's elves listen to as they work?

Wrap music.

December 25th

What's red and white and falls down chimneys?

Santa Klutz.

December 26th

What do you call a bankrupt Santa?

Saint Nickel-less!

December 27th

Where do snowmen go to dance?

To snowballs.

December 28th

What did the DNA say to the other DNA?

Do these genes make me look fat?

December 29th

What did the buffalo say to his sone when he dropped him off at school?

Bison!

December 30th

What did one snowman ask the other?

Do you smell carrots?

December 31st

Did you hear that Rudolph the Red-Nosed Reindeer never went to school?

He was elf-taught.

-- This page intentionally left blank --

-- This page intentionally left blank --

Check it out!

If you enjoyed this book, check out our other book:

Punny or Not Book of Puns
ISBN: 978-1951410049

Punny or Not Book of Puns is stuffed full of puns that are among the punniest of the funny. The question is: will you think they are punny or not? The best way to find out is to get your copy today!

There are sixteen categories of puns including:

- ➤ Cats and Dogs
- ➤ Food
- ➤ Wives
- ➤ People
- ➤ Fantasy
- ➤ Sports
- ➤ Space
- ➤ School
- ➤ And more!

Available on Amazon.com in both print and eBook formats!

Check it out!

For something fun, yet a little different:

Dots and Boxes Game
ISBN: 978-1951410063

Dots and Boxes is a fun game where players take turns connecting two dots in the hope of creating a box. The player that makes the most boxes by the end of the game is the winner!

The Dots and Boxes Game book contains a variety of playing boards that you can use. The book starts with several different sized standard gaming grids ranging from super small to a full page. These allow you to have play either a short game or a rather long one with a full-page grid.

The book also contains a variety of specialty game board based on different shapes. These range from simple shapes such as a cross and oval to more complex shapes such as a car, spider, flower, jet, train, and more.

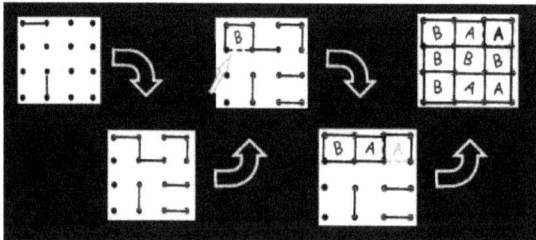

Available on Amazon.com today!

www.ingramcontent.com/pod-product-compliance
Lightning Source LLC
Chambersburg PA
CBHW071815020426
42331CB00007B/1489